A CENTURY of
SOUTHAMPTON

Located on the corner of Brunswick Place and Dorset Street, St Andrew's United Presbyterian/Congregational Church was completed in 1853 to serve the needs of Southampton's Presbyterian community and was always known as the 'Scottish Church'. In 1948, the church united with the congregation of the blitzed Above Bar Congregational Church (Isaac Watts' church). In the 1950s the church was also the home to the 7th Southampton troop of the Boys' Brigade. Although Grade II listed, the building was demolished in the late 1990s and replaced by Brunswick House, a modern block of offices. (*Crown Copyright NMR*)

A CENTURY of
SOUTHAMPTON

TONY GALLAHER

SUTTON PUBLISHING

First published in 2000 by Sutton Publishing Limited.

This new paperback edition first published in 2007 by
Sutton Publishing, an imprint of NPI Media Group
Cirencester Road · Chalford · Stroud · Gloucestershire · GL6 8PE

British Library Cataloguing in Publication Data
A catalogue record for this book is available from the British Library.

ISBN 978-0-7509-4901-9

Front endpaper: Southampton Docks in the early 1900s.
Back endpaper: The start of the Tall Ships race from Southampton in April 2000.
Half title page: Southampton's famous Bargate in 2000.
Title page: The Duke of Wellington, Southampton's oldest inn.

To my wife's aunt, Mrs Ada Cornforth, who was born in
Southampton in November 1899 and had lived in the city
throughout the entire twentieth century and into the twenty-first.
She sadly died in 2005, aged 105.

Typeset in 11/14pt Photina.
Typesetting and origination by
Sutton Publishing.
Printed and bound in England.

Contents

Queens Terrace, shown here in the 1970s, was the home for many maritime services in Southampton. At one time it had the Missions to Seamen hostel, the National Union of Seamen offices, several different offices for smaller shipping companies and the main office for the Marconi International Marine Communication Company. The latter was responsible for supplying radio equipment to the many ships that used the port; it also supplied the officers ('sparks') responsible for using and maintaining the equipment when at sea. Young officers joining the Merchant Navy could buy their complete sea-going uniforms from shops such as Baker's Shipping Branch on the corner of Queens Terrace and Latimer Street. On the right-hand side of the photograph, on the corner of Queens Terrace and Terminus Terrace, you can see Royal Mail House, which was once the head office of Royal Mail Lines; the building is still in use as offices. The whole area of Queens Terrace, Oxford Street, Bernard Street and Terminus Terrace is now listed as a conservation area. One of the most famous institutions in Queens Terrace was Tommy White's Restaurant at numbers 31 and 32 and is shown in the centre of the photograph. Value for money was Tommy White's motto and he certainly lived up to it. His reputation for good, no-frills food brought in customers from far and wide, although his main trade was feeding the hungry office workers from the many nearby shipping offices. He also had a licence to serve alcoholic drinks from six o'clock in the morning, which attracted many workers from the local fruit and vegetable markets. (*Gallaher Collection*)

Britain: A Century
of Change

Two women encumbered with gas masks go about their daily tasks during
the early days of the war. (*Hulton Getty Picture Collection*)

The sixty years ending in 1900 were a period of huge transformation for Britain. Railway stations, post-and-telegraph offices, police and fire stations, gasworks and gasometers, new livestock markets and covered markets, schools, churches, football grounds, hospitals and asylums, water pumping stations and sewerage plants totally altered the urban scene, and the country's population tripled with more than seven out of ten people being born in or moving to the towns. The century that followed, leading up to the Millennium's end in 2000, was to be a period of even greater change.

When Queen Victoria died in 1901, she was measured for her coffin by her grandson Kaiser Wilhelm, the London prostitutes put on black mourning and the blinds came down in the villas and terraces spreading out from the old town centres. These centres were reachable by train and tram, by the new bicycles and still newer motor cars, were connected by the new telephone, and lit by gas or even electricity. The shops may have been full of British-made cotton and woollen clothing but the grocers and butchers were selling cheap Danish bacon, Argentinian beef, Australasian mutton and tinned or dried fish and fruit from Canada, California and South Africa. Most of these goods were carried in British-built-and-crewed ships burning Welsh steam coal.

As the first decade moved on, the Open Spaces Act meant more parks, bowling greens and cricket pitches. The First World War transformed the place of women, as they took over many men's jobs. Its other legacies were the war memorials which joined the statues of Victorian worthies in main squares round the land. After 1918 death duties and higher taxation bit hard, and a quarter of England changed hands in the space of only a few years.

The multiple shop – the chain store – appeared in the high street: Sainsburys, Maypole, Lipton's, Home & Colonial, the Fifty Shilling Tailor, Burton, Boots, W.H. Smith. The shopper was spoilt for choice, attracted by the brash fascias and advertising hoardings for national brands like Bovril, Pears Soap, and Ovaltine. Many new buildings began to be seen, such as garages, motor showrooms, picture palaces (cinemas), 'palais de dance', and ribbons of 'semis' stretched along the roads and new bypasses and onto the new estates nudging the green belts.

During the 1920s cars became more reliable and sophisticated as well as commonplace, with developments like the electric self-starter making them easier for women to drive. Who wanted to turn a crank handle in the new short skirt? This was, indeed, the electric age as much as the motor era. Trolley buses, electric trams and trains extended mass transport and electric light replaced gas in the street and the home, which itself was groomed by the vacuum cleaner.

A major jolt to the march onward and upward was administered by the Great Depression of the early 1930s. The older British industries

– textiles, shipbuilding, iron, steel, coal – were already under pressure from foreign competition when this worldwide slump arrived. Luckily there were new diversions to alleviate the misery. The 'talkies' arrived in the cinemas; more and more radios and gramophones were to be found in people's homes; there were new women's magazines, with fashion, cookery tips and problem pages; football pools; the flying feats of women pilots like Amy Johnson; the Loch Ness Monster; cheap chocolate and the drama of Edward VIII's abdication.

Things were looking up again by 1936 and new light industry was booming in the Home Counties as factories struggled to keep up with the demand for radios, radiograms, cars and electronic goods, including the first television sets. The threat from Hitler's Germany meant rearmament, particularly of the airforce, which stimulated aircraft and aero engine firms. If you were lucky and lived in the south, there was good money to be earned. A semi-detached house cost £450, a Morris Cowley £150. People may have smoked like chimneys but life expectancy, since 1918, was up by 15 years while the birth rate had almost halved.

In some ways it is the little memories that seem to linger longest from the Second World War: the kerbs painted white to show up in the blackout, the rattle of ack-ack shrapnel on roof tiles, sparrows killed by bomb blast. The biggest damage, apart from London, was in the south-west (Plymouth, Bristol) and the Midlands (Coventry, Birmingham).

A W.H.Smith shop front in Beaconsfield, 1922.

Postwar reconstruction was rooted in the Beveridge Report which set out the expectations for the Welfare State. This, together with the nationalisation of the Bank of England, coal, gas, electricity and the railways, formed the programme of the Labour government in 1945.

Times were hard in the late 1940s, with rationing even more stringent than during the war. Yet this was, as has been said, 'an innocent and well-behaved era'. The first let-up came in 1951 with the Festival of Britain and there was another fillip in 1953 from the Coronation, which incidentally gave a huge boost to the spread of TV. By 1954 leisure motoring had been resumed but the Comet – Britain's best hope for taking on the American aviation industry – suffered a series of mysterious crashes. The Suez debacle of 1956 was followed by an acceleration in the withdrawal from Empire, which had begun in 1947 with the Independence of India. Consumerism was truly born with the advent of commercial TV and most homes soon boasted washing machines, fridges, electric irons and fires.

Children collecting aluminium to help the war effort, London, 1940s. (*IWM*)

The *Lady Chatterley* obscenity trial in 1960 was something of a straw in the wind for what was to follow in that decade. A collective loss of inhibition seemed to sweep the land, as the Beatles and the Rolling Stones transformed popular music, and retailing, cinema and the theatre were revolutionised. Designers, hairdressers, photographers and models moved into places vacated by an Establishment put to flight by the new breed of satirists spawned by *Beyond the Fringe* and *Private Eye*.

A street party to celebrate the Queen's Coronation, June 1953. (*Hulton Getty Picture Collection*)

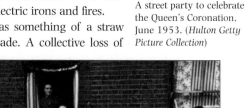

In the 1970s Britain seems to have suffered a prolonged hangover after the excesses of the previous decade. Ulster, inflation and union troubles were not made up for by entry into the EEC, North Sea Oil, Women's Lib or, indeed, Punk Rock. Mrs Thatcher applied the corrective in the 1980s, as the country moved more and more from its old manufacturing base over to providing services, consulting, advertising, and expertise in the 'invisible' market of high finance or in IT.

The post-1945 townscape has seen changes to match those in the worlds of work, entertainment and politics. In 1952 the Clean Air Act served notice on smogs and pea-souper fogs, smuts and blackened buildings, forcing people to stop burning coal and go over to smokeless sources of heat and energy. In the same decade some of the best urban building took place in the 'new towns' like Basildon, Crawley, Stevenage and Harlow. Elsewhere open warfare was declared on slums and what was labelled inadequate, cramped, back-to-back, two-up, two-down, housing. The new 'machine for living in' was a flat in a high-rise block. The architects and planners who promoted these were in league with the traffic engineers, determined to keep the motor car moving whatever the price in multi-storey car parks, meters, traffic wardens and ring roads. The old pollutant, coal smoke, was replaced by petrol and diesel exhaust, and traffic noise.

Fast food was no longer only a pork pie in a pub or fish-and-chips. There were Indian curry houses, Chinese take-aways and

Punk rockers demonstrate their anarchic style during the 1970s. (*Barnaby's Picture Library*)

American-style hamburgers, while the drinker could get away from beer in a wine bar. Under the impact of television the big Gaumonts and Odeons closed or were rebuilt as multi-screen cinemas, while the palais de dance gave way to discos and clubs.

From the late 1960s the introduction of listed buildings and conservation areas, together with the growth of preservation societies, put a brake on 'comprehensive redevelopment'. The end of the century and the start of the Third Millennium see new challenges to the health of towns and the wellbeing of the nine out of ten people who now live urban lives. The fight is on to prevent town centres from dying, as patterns of housing and shopping change, and edge-of-town supermarkets exercise the attractions of one-stop shopping. But as banks and department stores close, following the haberdashers, greengrocers, butchers and ironmongers, there are signs of new growth such as farmers' markets, and corner stores acting as pick-up points where customers collect shopping ordered on-line from web sites.

Millennium celebrations over
the Thames at Westminster,
New Year's Eve, 1999.
(*Barnaby's Picture Library*)

Futurologists tell us that we are in stage two of the consumer revolu-
tion: a shift from mass consumption to mass customisation driven by
a desire to have things that fit us and our particular lifestyle exactly,
and for better service. This must offer hope for small city-centre shop
premises, as must the continued attraction of physical shopping,
browsing and being part of a crowd: in a word, 'shoppertainment'.
Another hopeful trend for towns is the growth in the number of young
people postponing marriage and looking to live independently, alone,
where there is a buzz, in 'swinging single cities'. Their's is a 'flats-and-
cafés' lifestyle, in contrast to the 'family suburbs', and certainly fits in
with government's aim of building 60 per cent of the huge amount of
new housing needed on 'brown' sites, recycled urban land. There looks
to be plenty of life in the British town yet.

Southampton: An Introduction

The history of Southampton in the twentieth century shows it to be a town of constant change: if my grandmother were alive today, she would be hard-pressed to recognise it. Having expanded rapidly in the nineteenth century and the population reaching 104,000 in 1901, apart from the First World War, the first four decades of the twentieth century were relatively uneventful compared to the following six. The first electric trams were introduced in 1900, replacing the horse-drawn trams that began running in 1878, the Borough Hospital (now the General Hospital) opened in Shirley Warren in 1902 and the clearance of the slums in the old part of the town around Bugle and French Streets, under the Housing of the Working Classes Act of 1897, began in earnest in 1903.

No book on Southampton would be complete without a mention of one of the city's greatest tragedies. The White Star liner *Titanic*, having set sail from Southampton on her maiden voyage, struck an iceberg and sank with the loss of over 1,500 lives in April 1912. A memorial in the East Park to the ship's engineers, who remained at their stations for as long as possible while the ship was evacuated, was unveiled in 1914. (*Goddard Collection*)

Southampton was a major port for troop carriers and hospital ships during the First World War. Over seven million troops passed through the docks, but that didn't affect the face of the town, although commercial shipping was banned from the port for the duration, which caused some suffering for the townspeople. The town increased in population and area in the 1920s when Bitterne was included within the Borough. The 1920s was also the decade when Southampton was said to be the largest passenger port in the country and it foreshadowed the so-called 'Golden Age' of the 1930s when many large passenger liners used Southampton as their home port.

The demolition of buildings in Above Bar Street and the High Street so that the Bargate could be bypassed, the extension of the docks by the reclamation of land to the west, the beginning of the slum clearance in Kingsland and Orchard Lane and the opening of the Civic Centre were among the most significant acts that altered the look of the town in the 1930s. The slum clearance resulted in the building of some of the first council houses in the country, notably in Swaythling and Shirley Warren. The 1930s also saw the commencement of regular flying-boat services from Southampton Water. Southampton, through Vickers Supermarine, had had a connection with flying boats since about 1913. Sadly, the service ceased in the 1950s.

Many of the more radical changes to the town can be attributed to the Second World War because, like so many other British cities, Southampton

The sea defences of Southampton were built in the fourteenth century, mainly as a result of the French raid of 1338. Merchants' houses were incorporated into the town wall by a series of arcades. The photograph shows how it looked in the 1920s. (*Gallaher Collection*)

was very badly damaged in the blitz. The docks, the railways and the Vickers Supermarine Works at Woolston, where the first Spitfire fighter planes were built, were among the primary targets for the enemy. However, most of the medieval heart of the city was destroyed, taking with it much of Southampton's ancient history. The first raid was in June 1940 and the worst raids of all were on the night of 30 November/1 December 1940. After that there were more sporadic raids as German bombers passed over Southampton aiming for targets further inland. In fact, the Luftwaffe made about 57 raids on the town between 1940 and 1944. Apart from the severe damage that the German raids caused to the town, an estimated 630 citizens lost their lives.

1944 saw the arrival of the 'Yanks', which indicated that Southampton was going to be involved with the Normandy Landings. Three million troops passed though Southampton on their way to the Normandy beaches in June 1944 and two million of them were American. A plaque to commemorate the fact is on the memorial to the Pilgrim Fathers on the Western Esplanade.

Above Bar Street, East Street and High Street shopping and commercial centres were rebuilt in the early 1950s in an austere post-war style of architecture, due to a lack of imagination by the city planners, a lack of government funds and materials for postwar redevelopment. Work had also begun on rehousing bombed-out inhabitants in permanent accommodation. Such rebuilding brought the Millbrook, Harefield and Thornhill housing estates into the town boundaries, with Millbrook being the last to join in 1954. Having grown so much in a few years, Southampton was granted its city charter on

In the middle 1960s, Southampton aspired to becoming a major cross-channel ferry port. Here the first Townsend-Thoresen terminal is seen being built. The cross-channel service had mixed fortunes; various ferry companies tried to maintain a service but failed. Portsmouth and Poole are closer to France than Southampton, so those cities won the trade. (*Gallaher Collection*)

15

11 February 1964. It doesn't have a cathedral or a Lord Mayor like neighbouring Portsmouth but it is a city nevertheless.

With so many people living on the outskirts of the city, instead of residing within the city as they once did, the strain on the road systems into and out of the city worsened over the years. That, combined with an unprecedented increase in private transport, has led to much of the major redevelopment in the city since the end of the Second World War. People need roads to get them in and out of the city and also places to park their cars when they arrive at their destinations. It is this fact that has caused many of the extensive changes to Southampton in recent years.

Despite the damage that was done by the Germans, the medieval street plan remained virtually intact in 1945. However, in several acts of misguided redevelopment, the city street plan was changed beyond recognition in an effort to ease the flow of traffic. Castle Way (part of the Inner Ring Road, which no longer exists as such) was the result of the first such act; it cut a swathe through the old city wall, taking with it much of bomb-damaged, although historic, French Street, as well as the virtually undamaged Portland Terrace. Thankfully the Regency buildings in Portland Terrace were allowed to remain and have survived even the massive redevelopment work for the West Quay Shopping Mall, but the residential areas between Portland Terrace and the Western Esplanade fell victim to the planner's axe and were demolished. East Street was cut in half as a result of the demolition of the area around Orchard Lane and the creation of the Queensway part of the Inner Ring Road. A small alley known as Briton Street was widened to many times its original size to cater for the increase in traffic that resulted from the construction of the Inner Ring Road, which has since closed to through traffic. That act also caused the demolition of several more ancient buildings that had survived the bombing.

For over 40 years Vi Smith, selling her flowers on the corner of East Street and Queensway, has been a familiar sight in Southampton. She began trading in the courtyard of the Horse and Groom pub and moved to this place when the Horse and Groom was demolished in 1973.

Other recent road-improvement schemes in the city centre have caused the demise of the old Six Dials and the pretty Rose Gardens outside the Civic Centre. The Portswood, Swaythling and Bitterne areas of the city have been altered forever by their own traffic-improvement schemes.

Residential areas such as Northam and Chapel, where the houses were not of the highest quality but the people had a unique community spirit, were swept away in the 1960s and 1970s, together with many of the older parts of Shirley Warren and Bitterne. The Woolston area saw radical changes for the better in 1977 when the long-awaited Itchen Bridge replaced the old Floating Bridge, which first came into service in 1836. At the same time other parts of the city were also witnessing comprehensive changes. I have tried not to dwell entirely upon the scenes in the city centre; knowing that many Sotonians have fond memories of their roots, I have included several scenes from back streets in Chapel, Northam and other districts. Many of the streets depicted may be familiar only to the people who lived and worked in the area but they serve as useful reminders of how things were.

1997 saw the beginning of some far-reaching changes in the city's landscape as plans for the Southampton of the future were put into action. Demolition of the buildings to the west of Above Bar Street, including buildings in Portland Terrace and the Western Esplanade, began in October 1997 and the West Quay Shopping Mall, on the site of the old Pirelli cable factory, is on schedule to be completed in September 2000.

The new development will contain shops, cafés, restaurants, pubs, car parks and all the other amenities associated with a large city shopping centre. The demolition of the buildings between the Above Bar shopping precinct and the new development is expected to draw people to the new shops and transfer the focal point of the city to the west.

For hundreds of years, however, the focal point of the city has been the Bargate. Even the bombing of the Second World War could not alter that. All commercial development radiated from that old building from medieval times until the present day. I will not say that it is impossible to suddenly change such a focal point, but I wonder if the new development will work. I would hate to see the busy area around the Bargate become a 'ghost town' after so many years but I think the West Quay Shopping Mall will be a definite asset to the city.

Southampton has seen many changes over the years. It has always taken such changes in its stride and the people have adapted accordingly. Always a busy seaport, the city was important in the wool and wine trade in medieval times. When that trade dropped off, the city became a major spa resort, but when that business fell out of popularity, the railways had arrived and Southampton entered the most prosperous phase of its history. The coming of the railway meant that the Southampton docks could be expanded and the city soon grew into being the major passenger port in the country. The years that followed saw many famous passenger liners use the port. That period survived the Second World War but was killed off in the 1960s with the advent of cheap and reliable air travel.

After the demise of the liners, the city adapted to become a major container port for the (then) revolutionary container ships. A new container port was opened to the west of the existing docks in 1968 and this has proved very successful. Southampton docks now have a free trade zone and among the many items imported are motor vehicles. However, while the Western Docks survived as a base for P&O cruise liners, notably the *Arcadia*, the *Oriana* and the new *Aurora*, the Eastern Docks went into something of a decline, part of it ending up as the pleasant Ocean Village development of shops, houses, cinemas and marinas. The 31-year-old *Queen Elizabeth II* still uses the Eastern Docks, and the Eastern Docks saw the gathering of the tall ships in April 2000, so they do still have a role to play. Just to the east of the River Itchen is the Vosper-Thorneycroft shipyard in Woolston, which still provides shipbuilding work for many people.

Once part of the Inner Ring Road but now with traffic restrictions, Castle Way opened in about 1963 together with the Castle House apartment block. This photograph, taken in 1999, shows the 1960s architecture of the apartments contrasting with the fourteenth-century architecture of the old castle bailey.

Southampton's role as a major port and shipbuilder seems to remain undiminished. However, signs of the future indicate that Southampton will eventually become a dedicated 'University City'. Most new leisure development is aimed at people in their late teens and early twenties, the Southampton Institute continues to expand on its present site and has already taken over the old Plummer Roddis department store in Above Bar Street. Rumour has it that when Tyrrell and Green's store in Above Bar Street is relocated to its purpose-built new John Lewis premises in the West Quay Shopping Mall, the Southampton Institute has plans to take over the old building. The campus of the Southampton Institute could then extend from St Andrew's Road in the east to West Marlands Road in the west, and could also include some of East Park.

Southampton and its people have lived through their fair share of changes in the past. No doubt they will live through these changes too.

Edwardian Southampton

At the beginning of the twentieth century the picturesque old West Gate was still being used as a private dwelling. It wasn't until the 1930s that the roof was removed and the residents moved out. This photograph dates from about 1908 when Southampton Water still came within yards of the old walls. Dating back to the thirteenth century when it was built as part of the town's defences, the West Gate saw, among many other things, the departure of King Henry V and his troops on their way to Agincourt in 1415 and the departure of the Pilgrim Fathers to America in 1620. The building is now listed as an ancient monument. (*Gallaher Collection*)

Above Bar Street looks a tranquil, unhurried place in this photograph, which was taken in about 1908. The area was devastated during the German blitz of November 1940 and would now be unrecognisable to anyone who was alive at that time. On the left of the picture stands the Royal York Palace of Varieties, which dated back to the eighteenth century as a coaching inn called the Coach and Horses. The name changed to the Royal York Hotel in the 1830s and it became a full-time music hall in 1872. The original building was demolished in the 1890s and replaced by the building seen here. The entrance to the West Quay Shopping Mall stands on the site today. (*Gallaher Collection*)

Hansom cabs were still in use in Canute Road in the early 1900s. This photograph was taken in about 1901 and you can see the cabs waiting for passengers from the many ocean-going liners that used the port at that time. You can also see the South-Western Hotel in the background; the hotel was the best in Southampton in its time and provided accommodation for many important people travelling in and out of the town. It is interesting that most of the old buildings on the right still exist. (*Southern Newspapers plc*)

The Angel coaching inn in Bitterne village, *c*. 1900. The inn was an important stop on the route from Southampton to Portsmouth and had its own stables and carriage quarters. Dating back to the 1840s, the inn was demolished in August 1972 and today the site is occupied by Sainsbury's supermarket. (*Bitterne Local History Society*)

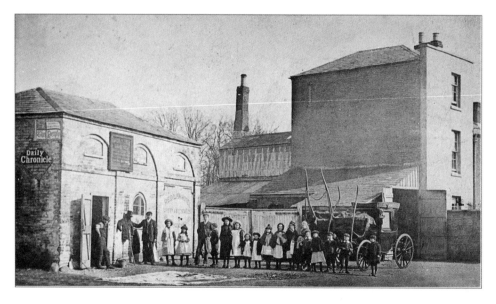

Just along the road from the Angel Inn was the Red Lion. That pub still exists and is the focal point of the Bitterne Shopping Precinct. This picture shows the pub's stables in about 1901 when, apparently, some Bitterne children were ready to go on an outing. (*Bitterne Local History Society*)

Many people remember the wooden Sun Hotel at the bottom of the High Street. It was the longest surviving 'temporary' building in the city. Not many photographs of the original building are known to exist, so the one shown is a rare example, taken in about 1900. The building dated back to the eighteenth century but, like the rest of that part of the High Street, it fell victim to the German bombing in 1940. (*Gallaher Collection*)

York Gate was not one of the original fourteenth-century gates into the city, having been added in the eighteenth century. This early twentieth-century view through the gate is to Hanover Buildings and the park beyond. Over the top of the gate were the gardens of Cooper's Brewery, whose main office you can see on the left. The gardens disappeared in about 1961 when the gate was demolished because it was a traffic hazard. The Georgian brewery office building still exists as part of the Bargate Centre shopping mall although at the time of writing the elegant building is unused but at least it's not derelict. (*Southampton Archives Services*)

Taken in about 1906, this view of the northern end of Southampton's elegant High Street shows many buildings that were destroyed in the blitz of 1940, including the Crown Hotel and All Saints Church on the right. Remarkably, the Bargate itself survived the bombing but the surroundings look very different in the twenty-first century. (*Gallaher Collection*)

The Avenue has been described as one the most beautiful entrances to any city in the country. This photograph shows The Avenue in the early years of the twentieth century after a heavy snowstorm. The scene is quite different in the twenty-first century: although the handsome trees still exist, the tram tracks and their associated overhead cables have long since gone and the traffic on the road, both into and out of the city, is something to be reckoned with. (*Gallaher Collection*)

This photograph, taken in about 1905, shows the number 18 open-top tram passing though the Bargate. Until the Bargate was bypassed in the 1930s, all trams had to go through the arch. That included the dome-topped trams which were designed especially to go through the Bargate, although rumour has it that the floor of the arch was lowered secretly and at night by the Town Engineers so that the dome-topped trams could pass through safely. (*Southampton Reference Library*)

The Platform, with Porters' Mead on the other side of the railway track, was once a popular place for bathing. This photograph, taken in about 1910, shows three young girls enjoying a paddle in the water. Porters' Mead was redeveloped to become Queen's Park and the South Western Hotel, in the background, served a postwar term as offices and has now been converted into luxury apartments. (*Southampton Reference Library*)

The residential areas of Southampton, such as Northam and Chapel, had an abundance of little pubs such as the Belvedere Arms shown here. The photograph was taken in about 1905 with landlord William Morey's daughters and some of his customers. The pub was known locally as the Mud and Duck because one of the landlords kept ducks on the muddy piece of spare ground seen on the left. (*Thorpe Collection*)

Tudor House Museum in Bugle Street is well known to residents of Southampton but it has been a museum only since 1912. This photograph, taken in about 1900, shows the house as a number of different residences and businesses, one of which was a laundry. The buildings on the right were demolished shortly after the photograph was taken, which widened Blue Anchor Lane and provided space for St Michael's House home for the homeless. (*Southampton Reference Library*)

25

Pembroke Square was a small cul-de-sac to the east of the Bargate. It was demolished in 1933 when the Bargate was bypassed. This photograph, taken on 25 April 1908, shows the square covered with four feet of snow after a freak snowstorm that happened that day. You can see Charles Kimber, landlord of the Pembroke Hotel (Kim's Kosy Korner), looking for any damage that the snowstorm may have caused to his property. (*Southampton Cultural Services*)

Southampton Central Station is the present name of the 1960s railway station on this site. When this photograph was taken in about 1901 it was known as Southampton West Station. It was also known as Blechynden Station; only later did it become Southampton Central Station, the name that it retains to this day. (*Gallaher Collection*)

The First World War
and the 1920s

Architect Sir Edwin Lutyens visited Southampton in 1919 to discuss with
the town council the design of a permanent memorial to the Southampton
people who had lost their lives in the First World War. The cenotaph in
Watts Park was unveiled on 6 November 1920 and was the inspiration for
the famous cenotaph in London's Whitehall. (*Gallaher Collection*)

British troops of the First World War are pictured here on an informal parade outside the Alexandra Hotel in Bellevue Road. In spite of extensive enquiries, I have been unable to identify either the regiment or the occasion. My guess, because it is obviously summertime, is that the soldiers were about to go to France in August 1914 at the start of the war. However, I do know that the landlord of the Alexandra Hotel at the time was Harry Chick, who you can see on the balcony of the hotel with his arms around a young lady. (*Southampton Cultural Services*)

The Northam area of Southampton was once famous for having a public house on the corner of each street. It wasn't strictly true but the area did have more than its fair share of pubs. Alfred Dowling became the landlord of the New Free House Inn in Northam's Peel Street in 1914. He is pictured here, in his shirtsleeves, with some of his family and his customers. (*Gallaher Collection*)

Even with the threat of war hanging over them, the people of Southampton went about their usual business in the summer of 1914. The top photograph shows the Bernard Street area, looking along Orchard Lane, with everyone dressed in their Sunday best. The lower picture, which may have been taken a bit before 1914, shows the customers of the Victoria Inn in Freemantle waiting to board their horse-drawn charabanc for their annual summer outing. (*Gallaher Collection*)

Southampton played a major part in the despatch of soldiers, transport, arms and provisions to France in 1914. Here a sorry-looking horse is being unceremoniously hoisted by crane aboard a troopship in Southampton docks in late 1914. It has been recorded that over 4,000 horses were exported from Southampton Docks on just one day in August 1914 as well as approximately 17,000 soldiers, 700 motor vehicles and over 250 bicycles. (*Southampton Archives Services*)

Captured German wounded soldiers were disembarked in Southampton Docks en route either to the internment camp in Shirley or, if seriously injured, to the Royal Victoria Hospital in Netley. The photograph shows 'walking-wounded' German prisoners of war arriving at Southampton Docks, probably on their way to the Royal Victoria Hospital and from there to a prisoner of war camp for the duration. (*Southampton Archives Services*)

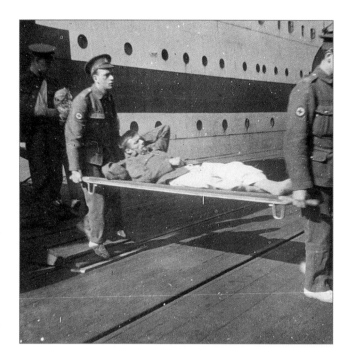

Many wounded British and soldiers from other countries came to England from France on hospital ships. These two photographs show wounded British soldiers being disembarked from a hospital ship in late 1914, probably en route to the Royal Victoria Hospital in Netley. (*Southampton Archives Services*)

No one appears to be taking notice of the group of German prisoners of war being marched up Shirley Road in 1917. Perhaps it was a common sight by then. The prisoners were on their way from Southampton Central Station to the temporary internment camp at the roller skating rink in Shirley before being sent to more permanent prisons elsewhere in the south of England. (*Southampton Archives Services*)

32

Group photographs were very popular in the early twentieth century. The top photograph shows the girls of Northam School in 1919 or 1920, while the lower picture shows the Peace Outing of Harland and Wolff plumbers on 12 July 1919. (*Southampton Archives Services*)

The Cowherds Inn is shown here in about 1915. Established in 1774 by cowherd Edwin Dyett, the pub has seen many, many changes over the years. It is the only pub actually on Southampton Common and so it is a popular place for a meal or a drink after a walk on the Common. (*Southampton Cultural Services*)

Bevois Valley Road, shown here in about 1915, has changed much in the years since the end of the Second World War. The tram rails were removed in the late 1940s, the Crown and Sceptre pub was bombed in the blitz and replaced by a new building in the 1950s, and the houses on the left were simply demolished. (*Southern Newspapers plc*)

This 1915 view of the south side of the Bargate shows how much the area changed in the twentieth century. Although attractive to look at, the Bargate was an obstacle to traffic. There wasn't much traffic to be seen in 1915 but in later years it became a real problem. Despite plans to dismantle the Bargate and sell it to the Americans, the old gate survived that and the blitz to become a main feature of the city. (*Gallaher Collection*)

The Station Hotel in Bitterne, shown here in about 1915, opened in about 1880 to serve passengers from trains that stopped at the nearby Bitterne railway station. The hotel still exists but has had many face-lifts over the years. (*Bitterne Local History Society*)

35

The disproportionately high spire of St Michael's Church was erected in the eighteenth century as a guide for ships coming into Southampton. The church itself, however, dates back to the thirteenth century. St Michael's Street is a fairly recent addition to the scene, dating from the latter half of the nineteenth century. The taxi rank still exists in the street and the National Provincial Bank building is still, arguably, one of the finest Victorian buildings in the city. Seen here in 1926, the spire of the church was undergoing some major restoration work. (*Southampton Reference Library*)

A procession of open-top motor cars took the Prince of Wales (later King Edward VIII) to open formally the first floating dry dock in the country in 1924. (*Southampton Archives Services*)

The world's largest floating dry dock, shown here in about 1926, was in service for many years and served famous Cunard liners such as the Majestic and the old Mauretania before being made redundant in 1933. (*Gallaher Collection*)

Seen here in the 1920s, London Road has always been a good-looking street. Unlike the present time, when the businesses are mainly estate agents and building societies, when this photograph was taken there were many different types of business operating in the street. On the right you can see St Paul's Church, which, together with the Unitarian Church just along the road, was destroyed in the blitz and never rebuilt. (*Gallaher Collection*)

The scene above shows a flat-topped tram (not designed to go though the Bargate) decked out as a 'football special' in 1928. The tram seems to be heading from Shirley towards London Road at the Town Junction: you can see Tudor buildings in the background. (*Southampton Reference Library*)

Henry Hartley, who died in 1850, owned a house on this site in the High Street. In his will he bequeathed a sum of money to go towards the founding of an educational institute in the town. Mr Hartley's house was replaced in the early 1860s by the building seen here. At first it was known as the Hartley Institute and then the Hartley College. The name changed to the Hartley University College in 1902 and then Southampton University in 1914 when it moved to the present site in Highfield. It became known officially as the University of Southampton in 1952. The old building was later used for many things – the photograph shows it in about 1926 when it was up for sale once again. (*Southampton Reference Library*)

The foundation stone of Mount Pleasant School was laid on 28 October 1896. This photograph shows a seemingly well-behaved mixed boys and girls infants' class in about 1923. (*Gallaher Collection*)

Porters' Mead, between the docks and Queen's Terrace, was laid out to become Queen's Park in the latter years of the nineteenth century. This early 1920s photograph shows the young trees and gardens that have since reached maturity and provide a pleasant little park right outside the dock gate. The park is dedicated to General Gordon of Khartoum; a monument was erected to him in the centre of the park in 1888. (*Gallaher Collection*)

East Street has always been one of the most popular shopping streets in Southampton. In the 1920s, however, when this photograph was taken, the street was not cut in two by Queensway and neither was it truncated by the East Street Shopping Centre. The photograph shows the High Street end of East Street with the elegant cupola of All Saints Church dominating the skyline. (*Southampton Reference Library*)

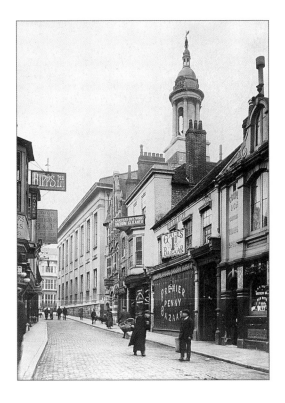

This photograph shows the St Mary Street end of East Street where it joined Marsh Lane. You can see Queens Buildings in the middle distance, which was the original home of Edwin Jones' department store. All the buildings in the top and bottom photographs were destroyed in the blitz of 1940. Very few original buildings remain in East Street in the twenty-first century. (*Southampton Reference Library*)

Hero of the Battle of Jutland during the First World War, Southampton-born Admiral Sir John Jellicoe was made a freeman of Southampton in 1926. This is his celebration procession going north along Above Bar Street, past the Royal Hotel on the right. (*Southampton Archives Services*)

Itchen Ferry was a small village back in the 1920s. Now absorbed into Woolston and unrecognisable, the area once had its own little shops, pubs and private houses. (*Gallaher Collection*)

All Saints Church burial ground was just off East Street and is shown here in about 1920. The bodies were removed and the ground deconsecrated after the church was destroyed in the blitz. The East Gate multi-storey car park now occupies the site. (*Southampton Reference Library*)

Unrecognisable in the twenty-first century, the Anchor and Hope still stands on the corner of Threefield Lane and Chandos Street. This photograph was taken in about 1925. (*Eldridge Pope*)

Few people remember Hawthorn Cottage on Southampton Common, pictured here in the middle 1920s. It was built on the site of a brick kiln in about 1814 by the then town clerk, Thomas Ridding. Evidently the circumstances surrounding the building of the cottage were a bit suspect because the land was meant to return to common use but, allegedly, strings were pulled and the cottage was built on the site. The second occupant was John Ransom, a prominent ship builder, and the final occupant was the widow of John Newman who took over the lease in about 1887. She lived there until her death in 1942. The Council bought the lease in 1945 but the house was in a sorry state after bomb damage and then being used by the army. The house was demolished in about 1946 and the grounds were used as a plant nursery by the Council and remained that way for years. In 1961, the Chipperfield family was given permission to erect a zoo on the site. The zoo, famous for James the smoking chimpanzee, was not all it should have been and in 1985 it was forced to close. The land lay idle for a few years until it was transformed into the Hawthorn Centre for natural wildlife on the Common in 1990. (*Crown Copyright NMR*)

The 1930s

The Clock Tower stood at the junction of New Road and Above Bar Street from the late 1880s until the middle 1930s when it was dismantled and moved to Bitterne Park Triangle, where it remains to this day. The Clock Tower was a bequest from a Mrs Henrietta Sayer whose will provided the funds for the clock and the drinking fountain below it. (*Gallaher Collection*)

The Bargate presented a major obstacle to the flow of traffic in the 1930s when private motor cars became increasingly popular. One of the more important problems was the fact that Southampton's tram car system allowed only for the trams to move through the Bargate arch. Dome-topped trams were developed to cope with the arch but, in the early 1930s, the town council took the decision to bypass the Bargate. Many old properties were demolished in the name of progress, including the Dickensian Pembroke Square which was on the left side of the north end of the Bargate. The photograph shows lots of people busy laying the tram tracks around the Bargate, but many were also spectators. New shops and offices were later built on the sites of the demolished buildings. (*Southampton Reference Library*)

This unusual view of the eastern side of the Bargate shows how it looked after the first phase of the bypass was finished. In about 1938 the western side of the Bargate was bypassed but, apart from replacing the centuries-old Bargate Hotel with a new building, redevelopment of the site did not really begin until after the end of the Second World War. (*Gallaher Collection*)

Early in the twentieth century the town council had outgrown its offices in the Audit House in the High Street, so the decision was made to construct new, purpose-built offices on the Marlands grounds. The project was master-minded by Alderman Sidney Kimber who became Sir Sidney Kimber in 1935. Here the Duke of York (later King George VI) is laying the foundation stone of the new building, the Civic Centre, on 1 July 1930. (*Southampton Archives Services*)

THE CIVIC CENTRE, SOUTHAMPTON. (20)   G.728.

These photographs, taken in about 1936, show the Civic Centre in its early days before the Guildhall and the Arts block were built – those buildings didn't arrive until about 1938. In the foreground of the photographs you can see the freshly planted and pretty rose garden that once enhanced the view of the Civic Centre. In 1987 the fountain was moved to its present site in front of the Art Gallery while the rose garden was ploughed over to widen Civic Centre Road and provide a new traffic system at the junctions of Civic Centre Road, Portland Terrace and Havelock Road. (*Gallaher Collection*)

Scullard's Hotel was established in about 1887 by Charles Scullard and was known then as Scullard's Adelaide Restaurant. The restaurant developed into a hotel and stayed in the Scullard family until the beginning of the twentieth century. The hotel shown above was demolished in the early 1930s and the Odeon Cinema was built on the site. Scullard then took over the White Hart Inn just a little way along Above Bar and renamed it accordingly. Those premises were bombed in 1940 and the later temporary premises were replaced by a brand-new building in 1953. The hotel in Above Bar Street shut for good in January 1973 but the name was resurrected for a short while in May 1986 for a bar in nearby Pound Tree Road. The 1953 hotel is still remembered by Scullard's Lane, which is just off Portland Street and runs parallel with Above Bar Street. (*Southern Newspapers plc*)

The Royal Yacht *Victoria and Albert* was the first ship to use the George V Graving Dock at the far end of Southampton's Western Docks. The dock is the largest of its kind in the world and was built especially for the maintenance of the large 80,000 tons plus Cunarders. This photograph shows the inauguration of the dock by King George V in 1935. (*Associated British Ports*)

The *Queen Mary* was the first Cunarder to use the new Graving Dock. This 1936 photograph shows her being pulled into place by tugs for her first lay-up. To celebrate the occasion, three ships in 107 to 109 berths are dressed overall, the ship in 108 berth being the *Majestic* which was scrapped the following year. (*Associated British Ports*)

Southampton Common is probably unique in the country. It passed into public ownership in the sixth century and has been cherished by Sotonians ever since. Although largely unchanged from the scenes of the twenty-first century, these photographs from the middle 1930s show many of the subtle differences that have occurred. The top photograph is of a bunch of youths in what was then called Lovers' Walk at the north end of the Common. The Common was, and probably still is, a popular venue for courting couples. The lower photograph shows the Yacht Pond in the 1930s when it was still Southampton's 15-foot deep third reservoir. It wasn't until 1945 that the depth was lowered to the present four feet. (*Gallaher Collection*)

The manufacture of seaplanes and flying boats began in the Vickers Supermarine Works at Woolston in about 1913 and the first flying boat, a PB1, was launched early in 1914. The Vickers Supermarine Works was better known for one of its most famous sons, R.J. Mitchell, who designed the Supermarine S6 seaplane (above) which won the Schneider Trophy in 1931. (*Southampton Archives Services*)

Building on the success of the design of his seaplane, R.J. Mitchell went on to design and develop the world-famous Supermarine Spitfire fighter. The Spitfire seen here is a prototype being put through its paces in March 1936. Sadly, R.J. Mitchell died on 11 June 1937 but development of the Spitfire continued and, with its official top speed of 349 miles per hour, played a vital part in defeating the Luftwaffe in the Battle of Britain in 1940. As a tribute to R.J. Mitchell, a Mitchell Museum was later set up on a site on the Marlands. The museum is now in Albert Road, where a genuine Spitfire is on display among many other reminders of Southampton's important aviation history. (*Woolston Camera Club*)

Two picturesque views of the city walls in the 1930s. The top view shows the monument to the Pilgrim Fathers and several cannon that were captured in the Crimean War. The cannon were scrapped to help the war effort in the 1940s and were never replaced. The lower view shows Arundel Tower and Catchcold Tower with the Forty Steps to the right. The buildings and trees have gone but otherwise the old walls are much the same. (*Gallaher Collection*)

As the docks in Southampton expanded, so also did the need for a pier to handle smaller craft to and from the Isle of Wight. The first Royal Pier was opened in 1833 by the then Princess Victoria and named after her – at first it was known as the Royal Victoria Pier but the name soon became shortened to the Royal Pier. Over the years the pier was extended and altered beyond recognition until it was rebuilt in 1891. Although they still exist, the entrance pillars to the 1891 pier are in a different position to that intended and the domed entrance to the pier, which was erected in the late 1920s, a year or two before the above photograph was taken, still exists. In the 1950s and the 1960s, the Mecca Ballroom at the end of the pier enjoyed immense success as a dancing venue for young people. The ballroom was destroyed by fire on 5 April 1987 and was never rebuilt. The domed gatehouse ceased to be a ticket office for Isle of Wight ferries about the same time. The gatehouse later became a bar/nightclub but it changed hands several times and is now derelict, as indeed is the whole of the Royal Pier. (*Gallaher Collection*)

Taken in the late 1930s, this photograph shows the ever-popular Lido in the Western Esplanade. Swimming baths, in one form or another, had been on this site for decades. The Lido was popular with Sotonians right through to its demise in the 1970s. The site lay derelict for several years until it was redeveloped to make way for the Asda Supermarket car park. (*Gallaher Collection*)

Behind Southampton's elegant High Street and
Above Bar Street stood many mean streets, alleys
and courtyards. This pair of photographs, from
about 1933, shows the conditions in Challis
Court, which was just off Orchard Lane. Note
the tin baths on the wall: the people may have
been poor but they were clean. Most of Challis
Court was demolished in the early 1930s, the
blitz took care of some more buildings and the
courtyard was finally demolished in the middle
1950s. (*Southampton Archives Services*)

Also off Orchard Lane stood Bell Street which, in the 1930s, ran up to Canal Walk. You can see the Lord Roberts public house at the end of the road. Now called The Strand, it is the only building in the picture that still exists. (*Southampton Archives Services*)

Lime Street, shown here in about 1933 before demolition, was also just off Orchard Lane. Most of this area is now apartment blocks. (*Southampton Archives Services*)

Just a stone's throw from Orchard Lane stood Queen Street. This photograph, looking north along the street into Lime Street, was taken in about 1933. The street and the surrounding area were demolished shortly afterwards. (*Southampton Archives Services*)

Threefield Lane runs parallel with Orchard Lane and was also subject to slum clearance in the early 1930s. Like Orchard Lane, Threefield Lane had many courtyards and small alleys attached. This photograph, taken in about 1933, shows six children in Wheelers Court, dressed in their Sunday best especially for the camera. (*Southampton Archives Services*)

These photographs of each end of Sawmill Court, which was just off Threefield Lane, show how run down the area was in the 1930s. Small businesses, such as the old bicycle shop on the corner of Sawmill Court and Threefield Lane, were still plentiful but the trade could not have been very good. Along with most of the other buildings in the area, these buildings were demolished in the slum clearance of the early 1930s. (*Southampton Archives Services*)

Judd's Newsagent and Confectionery shop and Metcalfe's Jubilee Stores stood on the corner of St Mary Street and Chapel Street. Together with many of the older buildings in the lower part of St Mary Street, the building was demolished in the middle 1930s and replaced by a more modern building that later housed Reema and Company, General Dealers. (*Southampton Archives Services*)

Looking up Johnson Street into St Mary Street, you can see Bigland's bakery. Although most of the buildings seen here were demolished in the slum clearance of the 1930s, the view to Bigland's from what is left of Johnson Street is the same in the twenty-first century. Bigland's is still a bakery and the shop front is exactly the same as it was all those years ago. (*Southampton Archives Services*)

Between St Mary Street, North Front, South Front and Palmerston Road (once known as West Front) stood a motley of ramshackle shops, public houses and dwellings that formed the Kingsland area of Southampton. This photograph shows Craven Street, one of the major streets, in the early 1930s. One of the two women chatting is leaning on what was once the Carpenter's Arms public house, on the corner of Craven Street and Nightingale Court. The Kingsland area was among the first to go in the slum clearances of the 1930s. The area was redeveloped with council flats in the 1950s but had lain empty during the war years, the only two remaining landmarks then being the spire of Trinity Church in North Front and the Greyhound pub in Cossack Street (now Cossack Green). (*Southampton Archives Services*)

Like so many other of the poor areas of the town, Kingsland had its maze of courtyards and alleys. This one was called Cossack Place and consisted of a small alley just off Cossack Street. (*Southampton Archives Services*)

It's hard to believe that as recently as the 1930s poor housing such as this existed in Spa Road, on the site of what is now the Above Bar Street entrance to the prestigious West Quay Shopping Mall. These houses were demolished in the 1930s but nothing became of the land until the 1950s because of the intervention of the Second World War. (*Southampton Archives Services*)

Rehousing of the many people who had lost their homes because of the slum clearance in the 1930s was uppermost in the minds of the town planners. The council acquired a large amount of land to the north of the town and built what was among the first real council estates in the country. To this day known as 'the flower roads', Bluebell Road, Lilac Road, Primrose Road and so on were built in the Bassett/Swaythling areas in the late 1920s and the early 1930s to rehouse the people. J.C.Holly, a builder from Adelaide Road, was responsible for the construction of many of the houses – the group photograph shows Mr Holly (on the far left) with his team of workers in the early 1930s, when the houses were being built. (*Haskell Collection*)

The Second World
War and the
Postwar Years

The fiercest wartime air raids on Southampton occurred in November and
December 1940. The centre of the town was devastated to such an extent
that King George VI visited the town to inspect the damage personally. He
is seen here with the Mayor of Southampton and the Chief Health Officer
walking along Above Bar Street in December 1940. (*Southampton Archives
Services*)

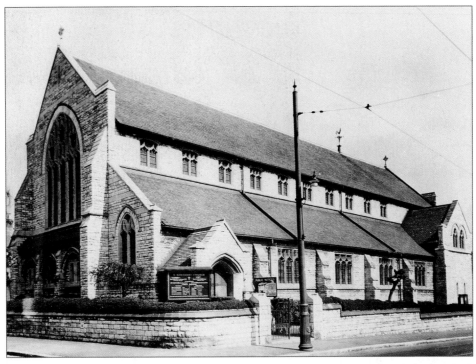

Located on the corner of Lodge Road and Rose Road, St Barnabas Church received a direct hit by a land mine shortly after this photograph was taken in September 1940. The site became an unofficial adventure playground for all the local children until the late 1950s when the present building was erected. (*Southampton Archives Services*)

This Central Girls' School class of 1940 was probably one of the last groups to be photographed before wartime restrictions began. (*Southampton Archives Services*)

The British American Tobacco warehouse was among the many buildings completely destroyed in the raids of November and December 1940. In this scene firemen are still damping down the blaze. (*Southampton Archives Services*)

The ruins of London Road, as seen from the corner of London Road and Bellevue Road in early 1941. Just the facade of Lloyd's Bank, a few chimney stacks and a solitary fire escape remain. (*Southampton Archives Services*)

Two views of French Street in 1941 show the damage that was done to the historic medieval heart of Southampton. In the top photograph, the building on the right has since been restored to become a museum. The rest of French Street was not as fortunate. The lower photograph shows the ruins of the house where Isaac Watts, composer of 'O God Our Help In Ages Past', once lived. The building was too badly damaged to be restored. (*Southampton Archives Services*)

Two unrecognisable streets in the Northam area of the city show how badly the homes of ordinary working people were affected by the blitz. (*Southampton Archives Services*)

In spite of everything, small boys found the bomb sites to be great places to play. This photograph shows two boys playing on a site in Earls Road in about 1943. (*Southampton Archives Services*)

The Old Farm House pub in Mount Pleasant Road looks very sorry for itself, 11 July 1941. The houses on the opposite side of the road were destroyed in an air raid but the pub was undamaged except that all the tiles came off the roof. You can see them stacked neatly in piles ready to be put back into place. (*Crown Copyright NMR*)

Both taken on 24 June 1942, the top photograph is of the Star Hotel and surrounding buildings in the High Street. The bombing exposed a maze of medieval vaults, which you can see in the foreground. The bottom photograph is the view from the roof of the Star Hotel across the ruins to the Zion Chapel, which stood on the site of Castle House in what is now Castle Way. (*Crown Copyright NMR*)

This photograph, taken in about 1943, is of the blitzed ruins of Holy Rood Church, now dedicated to the merchant seamen of Southampton. It also includes a memorial fountain to seamen who lost their lives on the *Titanic*: the memorial fountain used to be on Southampton Common but was moved to Holy Rood some years ago. (*Southampton Archives Services*)

Taken in about 1945, this general view of the High Street shows how much of the western side was destroyed in the blitz. The scene looks very drab and dreary; even the trams are still in their wartime grey livery. Only the Dolphin Hotel looks the same then as it is today. (*Southern Newspapers plc*)

In this rare photograph of the two 'Queens', taken in 1946, you can see on the right the *Queen Mary*, still in the battleship grey of the war, and the *Queen Elizabeth* on the left, refitted and ready to start on her first commercial voyage to New York. Both ships had served as troop carriers during the war and although the *Queen Mary*'s maiden voyage was in 1936 and she did serve time as a commercial liner, the *Queen Elizabeth*, being launched in 1938, was carrying troops as soon as the war began. (*Southampton Archives Services*)

Southampton's history of flying-boat development before the Second World War prompted postwar attempts to introduce a permanent flying-boat service to and from Southampton. Aquila Airways was one that made a brave attempt to establish a regular service: you can see one of its flying boats landing a cargo of apricots in May 1949. (*Associated British Ports*)

Built in about 1802 and named after Earl Moira whose troops were once stationed in Southampton, Moira Place, at the junction of New Road and Above Bar Street was originally a private dwelling. It was just one of a number of such private dwellings that had been built in Above Bar Street as the city expanded in the late eighteenth and early nineteenth centuries. As the commercial heart of Southampton slowly moved beyond the boundaries of the old town walls, the building later had many other uses. By 1945, when this photograph was taken, the old building had been extended and served as the offices of the Co-operative Permanent Building Society. On the green to the right of the offices you can see part of the National Savings 'thermometer'. In an attempt to encourage people to save during the war years, each week the 'thermometer' changed to show the people of Southampton how much money they had invested in National Savings to help the war effort. The photograph shows that £15,283,290 had been saved so far! The 'thermometer' disappeared in the 1950s and Moira Place was demolished in the 1960s to be replaced by the flat, square building that is there now. (*Crown Copyright NMR*)

Captain Peacock was a master mariner who discovered anti-fouling for protecting ships' bottoms. He patented the idea and, with the help of a Mr Buchan, established the Peacock and Buchan paint factory in Oakley Road in 1848. One hundred years later the firm celebrated the centenary with a coach outing. Mr Yeoman, the factory manager, is the fierce-looking gentleman sixth from the left in the front row and Mr Bicknell, head storeman, is on the far right of the front row. Mr Bicknell was also the chairman of the local branch of the Old Contemptibles Association. (*Southampton Archives Services*)

The first postwar Bevois Town School outing was to Henley-on-Thames in the summer of 1949. War-time clothing coupons had been abolished by then but the lads seen here are hardly a picture of sartorial elegance. Times were still hard in those days. (*Gallaher Collection*)

Outlook BRIGHTER!

THE TAILORING POSITION
is improving: Coupon restrictions have been removed, clothes are becoming more plentiful, and Baker's can now offer you a suit, tailored to your individual measurements and tailored by expert craftsmen in 14 days if necessary.

Also the ready-made clothing departments of our Southampton branches are better equipped to deal with your needs in Boys' and Men's Clothing of Baker **QUALITY** . . . such as a Baker's ready-to-wear suit . . . and know at once that quality, style, cut—and price—are *right* for you. Baker's have a wide range of styles and materials . . . and every garment enjoys that permanency of shape and long life which comes from only the most painstaking workmanship.

When next you require a fitting of any kind—remember, Baker's have a special branch for your son—you will find your call at a Baker's Branch both pleasurable and profitable.

Baker & Co
J. Baker & Co. Ltd.

MEN'S & BOYS' OUTFITTERS

Branches at

53/56 East Street, Southampton
104 East Street, Southampton
53/55 High Street, Shirley, Southampton
11 Leigh Road, Eastleigh, Southampton
18 Portsmouth Road, Woolston, Southampton
AND AT PORTSMOUTH

Head Office: 70 Commercial Road, Portsmouth

Shipping Branches: Southampton, Liverpool, Avonmouth, Royal Albert & Tilbury Docks, London

R.N. Branches: Portsmouth, Devonport, Portland, Chatham

This contemporary advertisement from 1948 was for J. Baker & Co., which had several shops in Southampton, including a large shop at the lower end of East Street and another large shop on the corner of Church Street and Shirley High Street. The advertisement makes a point of saying that clothing coupons were no longer necessary to buy new clothes. Not many people today would care to be seen in a suit such as the one advertised, but fashions change and I daresay that the suit advertised was a vast improvement on the 'demob suits' issued in 1945. (*Gallaher Collection*)

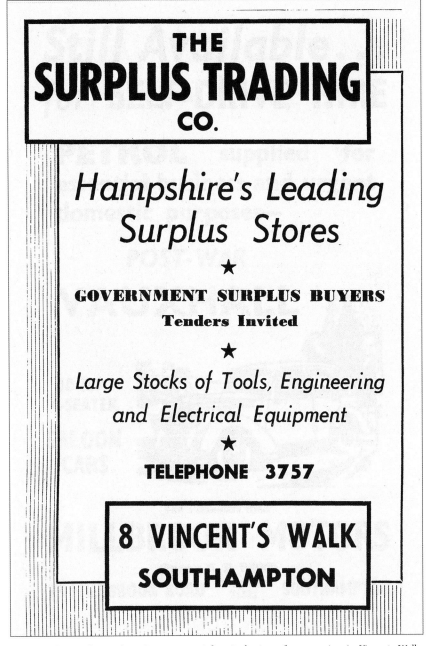

THE SURPLUS TRADING CO.

Hampshire's Leading Surplus Stores

★

GOVERNMENT SURPLUS BUYERS

Tenders Invited

★

Large Stocks of Tools, Engineering and Electrical Equipment

★

TELEPHONE 3757

8 VINCENT'S WALK SOUTHAMPTON

In 1948, the Surplus Trading Company carried on its business from premises in Vincents Walk. Since about 1953, Vincents Walk, which runs parallel with the Above Bar Shopping Precinct, was used mostly for the rear entrances to the major stores. What the German bombs missed in 1940 was demolished in the early 1950s when Above Bar Street was rebuilt. (*Gallaher Collection*)

Still Available...
for SELF-DRIVE HIRE

PETROL supplied for essential business and urgent domestic purposes—

POST-WAR

VAUXHALL

10-H.P. 4-SEATER

SALOON CARS

Full Particulars from

MILLBROOK MOTORS

(Propr. : H. E. WORT)

75 MILLBROOK ROAD   Telephone 71433   SOUTHAMPTON

In the immediate postwar years, petrol was still hard to get and a motor car was still a luxury. This 1948 advertisement for Millbrook Motors seems to offer a solution to the problem. (*Gallaher Collection*)

The 1950s and
the 1960s

This aerial view of the Western Docks in the late 1950s shows how busy
Southampton once was as a passenger port. In the foreground, alongside
101 Berth, are three Union Castle liners. Alongside 102 Berth is yet
another Union Castle liner, tied up to the Holland America Line *Rotterdam*,
which entered service in September 1959. The *Rotterdam* is still in service
as an American-owned cruise liner but has since been renamed the
Rembrandt. (*Associated British Ports*)

Although they now seem to be a thing of the past, youth clubs were very popular in the 1950s. They provided young people with a good way of making new friends and offered facilities such as darts, dances and billiards. The photograph shows the St Barnabas Youth Club outing to Littlehampton in 1955. Other popular clubs were the Teen and Twenty Club in Portswood and the Ashby Youth Club in Shirley. (*Gallaher Collection*)

Bernard Street in the early 1950s still showed signs of the devastation of war. Most of the buildings that survived the war were later demolished to make way for offices and council flats. The only recognisable feature in the photograph is the spire of St Michael's Church in the distance. (*Veal Collection*)

Compton Walk ran from East Park Terrace to St Mary's Road. It was demolished in the 1960s and the Charlotte Place car park and traffic circle has occupied most of the site since. This photograph was taken in the late 1950s when the Gospel Witness Fellowship (the Bible Shop) still had its premises at the top end of the road. (*Southampton Archives Services*)

Not far away from Compton Walk stood St Matthew's Mission Hall, on the corner of Dorset Street and Bellevue Street. This is a view from the late 1950s and the hall was demolished, together with many of the surrounding properties, in the 1960s. A modern office block was erected on the site in the 1970s. (*Southampton Archives Services*)

The first grammar school to be funded by Richard Taunton was established in Windsor Terrace in 1760. This building iwas the second school; it was in New Road and opened in 1865. Taunton's Grammar School moved to new premises in Highfield in 1926 and the New Road building later became the Southampton Charitable Dispensary and Dental Institution. Although the building was spared when the town was bombed during the blitz, all buildings in the area have since been demolished to allow for the continuing expansion of the Southampton Institute, which now occupies the site. (*Veal Collection*)

This building began life as the Southampton Grammar School for Girls in Hill Lane in 1926, having moved from Argyle Road. As times changed and the education structure changed with it, the school became Hill Sixth Form College. With the closure of Taunton's Grammar School in Highfield, the name was transferred here so that it is now known as Taunton's College. This photograph was taken in about 1950 when it was still the Southampton Grammar School for Girls, but I doubt that the garden and fountain are still there. (*Southampton Archives Services*)

These two photographs show how the southern side of Northam Road, a main road into and out of the city, looked in the 1950s. The road was largely spared during the blitz but fell victim to the planner's axe in the middle 1950s. Both photographs show how the road was made up of small shops, many of which were grocers, butchers or cycle shops. The bottom picture shows the office of Avery, the scale-making business, whose repair depot was in St Mary Street, but even that office had to share premises with a butcher's shop. (*Southampton Archives Services*)

The Plaza cinema was still in existence when the present Northam Bridge was being constructed in 1953. The scene is very different in the twenty-first century: the 1953 Northam Bridge is still there but the studios of Meridian Television currently occupy the site of the Plaza. (*Veal Collection*)

There was a time when South Front was a collection of contrasting styles of architecture. This photograph, taken in about 1955, shows the many different styles that had evolved over the years and also includes the local office of the *News of the World*. The buildings were all demolished in the 1970s and replaced by apartment buildings. (*Southampton Archives Services*).

Different types of temporary buildings abounded in Southampton in the 1950s. The top photograph was taken in about 1956 and shows the temporary premises of the Plummer Roddis Department Store. The temporary building was replaced by a permanent one in 1958 but has since closed for business, now being part of the Southampton Institute. The bottom photograph shows the area around Central Station in 1954, with Nissen huts on the site of the bombed buildings around Blechynden Terrace and a temporary pub in the middle distance. The photograph was taken from the footbridge that still exists over the railway line. (*Veal Collection*)

Taken from the High Street, these two views show how the area around St Michael's Church looked in the early 1950s. The top photograph shows the church as it looked from the corner of the High Street and West Street, while the bottom photograph provides a more general view of the area and includes scenes of the postwar reconstruction work that was going on at the time. All the older buildings in both pictures were demolished in the early 1960s when the now redundant Inner Ring Road was constructed. (*Veal Collection*)

School outings were popular in the 1950s. This photograph shows Western Secondary Modern School's visit to the Houses of Parliament on 22 March 1954. George Reader, the headmaster at the time, is in the centre. He was acquainted with Dr Horace King, the Southampton Itchen MP, who you can also see in the centre of the photograph. Dr King went on to become the Speaker of the House of Commons and later received a peerage to become Lord Maybray-King. (*Gallaher Collection*)

Apart from schools, many businesses had annual outings for their workers. This is the staff outing of Poupart's Fruit and Vegetable Wholesaler to Bognor Regis in the summer of 1952. (*Bromby Collection*)

These two views of Tudor House Museum in the middle 1950s show it as a well-established centre of attraction in St Michael's Square. The house was built for Sir John Dawtry of Petworth in the early sixteenth century and later became the home of Sir Richard Lyster, Chief Baron of the King's Exchequer during the reign of Henry VIII. Evidently Henry was a regular guest at the house and, so the story goes, Anne Boleyn once stayed there with him. (*Southampton Archives Services*)

Prefabricated houses (prefabs) for those people whose own homes had been destroyed during the blitz were prevalent in many parts of the town in the 1950s. Although small, they provided ample accommodation for the homeless and they also had built-in refrigerators, a luxury unheard of in the 1950s. These prefabs were in Priory Road, St Denys. (*Bromby Collection*)

Although taken in 1997, this photograph shows a housing development typical of the late 1950s. These particular flats are in French Street and are built over the top of old Norman vaults. You can find other examples of this type of bland 1950s architecture in the Orchard Lane area.

85

The Ocean Terminal is shown here in the middle 1950s. United States Line's Blue-Riband holder *United States* is tied up alongside. Prime Minister Clement Attlee opened the Ocean Terminal in 1950. The terminal catered for the passengers on the transatlantic service and included baggage handling, shops, cafés and bars. With the demise of the transatlantic liners, the building became redundant and was demolished in 1983. (*Associated British Ports*)

Number 9 shed in the Eastern Docks is shown in 1953, decorated for the coronation of Queen Elizabeth II. In later years this shed fell into disuse but found a new life in the 1980s as Canute's Pavilion in Ocean Village. (*Associated British Ports*)

The Korean War ended in 1953. These are repatriated British prisoners of war disembarking at Southampton Docks later that year. (*Associated British Ports*)

The *Queen Elizabeth* is alongside Berth 107, while in the foreground is the site of what was to become the largest undersea cable manufacturer in the world. The two factories of Standard Telephones and Cables were erected on this site: one in the 1950s and the other in the 1960s. In 1963 the company claimed that it could supply a complete transatlantic cable, with 128 voice circuits, in less than a year. (*Associated British Ports*)

In the early 1950s, Southampton aspired to become a large fruit and vegetable market, on a par with Covent Garden in London. T.J. Poupart, which was already established in Southampton, opened its new offices and warehouses on the site of the Hartley Institute in the High Street. The building was among the first to be built in the war-damaged High Street but was demolished in 1999 to make way for luxury apartments. (*Veal Collection*)

This view of East Street, looking along the Strand and into Canal Walk in the early 1950s, has the notorious Horse and Groom public house as its main feature. The pub was known to seafarers the world over; it was often the scene of fights and even killings. It remained in the same family from the early 1900s until it was demolished in 1973. (*Southampton Archives Services*)

The left-hand side (going north) of Bevois Valley Road actually had houses and small shops in the early 1960s. The photograph shows a line of such premises that were demolished around that time. The whole of that side of the road, from Earls Road to Forster Road, is now occupied by second-hand car dealers. (*Southampton Archives Services*)

In the early 1960s, Bitterne Road, although still busy, was nowhere near as busy as it is today. Not much traffic can be seen and the Manor Stores corner shop was still in business. The widening of the road later in the 1960s meant that many of the properties in this picture had to be demolished. (*Southampton Archives Services*)

This busy docks scene in about 1958 is typical of Southampton docks during that time. In the photograph you can see stevedores going about unloading cargo fresh from South Africa from the Union Castle liner *Edinburgh Castle*. (*Associated British Ports*)

The Ordnance Survey map-making offices were established in Southampton's London Road in 1841. The handsome old buildings were subjected to severe damage during the blitz of 1940 but were shored up to continue with the work to assist the war effort. New premises were needed, however, and on 1 May 1969, Her Majesty Queen Elizabeth II formally opened the purpose-built new headquarters at Maybush. The site, shown here just after it had opened, has expanded very much over the years and the data gained by the Ordnance Survey now is so valuable that around £100 billion worth of economic activity in Britain is dependent on it. Most of the old Ordnance Survey buildings in London Road were demolished in the 1980s and Southampton's new Magistrates' Court was erected on the site. (*Ordnance Survey*)

The view along Bargate Street in the early 1960s changed dramatically when Castle Way, the Inner Ring Road, was constructed in about 1963. The photograph shows the old Pirelli cable factory at the bottom end of Bargate Street, with the Olde Arundel Tower Inn on the corner. The Inner Ring road was closed to traffic in 1997 and it is unlikely ever to open again. (*Veal Collection*)

A 1960s view of the Western Esplanade shows part of the Pirelli factory and the popular Southampton Lido. Development of the eastern side of the road (mainly car parks) had begun in earnest by then. In the distance you can see the two chimneys of the long-gone power station that was opposite the main railway station. (*Veal Collection*)

The row of small shops that were in the part of St Mary's Road that led from Brintons Terrace to Onslow Road is shown here in the 1960s. The area later became really run down and several of the individual shop premises were merged into one to become a nightclub. (*Veal Collection*)

The lower end of the High Street was completely destroyed in the blitz of 1940. Where there was once a row of medieval buildings there was nothing but a collection of bomb sites. Rather than build on the medieval sites, the area was landscaped and transformed into the Town Quay Park in 1963. (*Southampton Archives Services*)

Grosvenor Square Garages and the Milton Coach Works were one and the same. But that didn't stop the company publishing two separate advertisements in the 1962 issue of *Kelly's Street Directory*. However, it is good to see an old Vauxhall Victor in the top advertisement and a lovely Ford Zodiac in the lower one. (*Gallaher Collection*)

A.A.   R.A.C.

GROSVENOR SQUARE GARAGES

PETROL   ✦   OILS   ✦   SERVICING
GARAGING   ✦   CAR PARK
SELF-DRIVE (J. DAVY CAR HIRE LTD.)

GROSVENOR SQUARE - SOUTHAMPTON

Telephone: Southampton 20854 & 28777

MILTON COACH WORKS CO.

(A. SMITH)

SPECIALISTS
IN
PANEL
BEATING
CELLULOSING
WELDING

BODY AND
CHASSIS
REPAIRS

COACH
TRIMMING

CHROMIUM
PLATING

Contractors to the Motor Trade, Leading Garages and Insurance Companies for Accident Damage

SELF-DRIVE (J. DAVY CAR HIRE LTD.)

2 GROSVENOR SQUARE - SOUTHAMPTON

PHONE: SOUTHAMPTON 20854 & 28777

The graceful *Queen Mary*'s maiden voyage from Southampton was in 1936. In October 1967 she left Southampton for the last time, bound for California where she became a floating hotel and conference centre. A 31-foot paying-off pennant flying from her after mast marks her 31 years in service. (*Southern Newspapers plc*)

The very first B&Q DIY shop in England was opened in Portswood Road in 1969. The building was once a meeting hall, sometimes used as a cinema. B&Q stands for Block and Quayle, the names of the two founding members of the enormously successful DIY company. (*B&Q*)

The 1970s and
the 1980s

The few shops at the lower end of East Street missed the worst damage of the wartime blitz, unlike the rest of the street, which was completely destroyed. In the late 1970s, however, the few remaining old buildings were demolished and the East Street Shopping Centre mall was erected on the site, making East Street into a cul-de-sac. Many of the shops in the mall have changed hands over the years and I am not sure that the mall is the success that it was intended to be. This photograph was taken in about 1982, when it was still possible to park your car near the shops. (*Southampton Reference Library*)

Despite being one of the hottest summers in living memory, as far as Southampton was concerned the highlight of 1976 was when the Saints football team beat Manchester United to win the FA cup at Wembley. The photograph shows the team's formal line-up when it received the freedom of the city for its achievement. In the front row, from left to right, are Mike Channon, Paul Gilchrist, Jim McCalliog, Lawrie McMenemy (manager), Peter Rodrigues (captain), Barry Stokes and David Peach. In the back row, from left to right, are Jim Clunnie (trainer), Pat Earls, Nick Holmes, Jim Steele, Peter Osgood, Ian Turner, Hugh Fisher, Mel Blyth and Paul Bennett. (*Southampton Archives Services*)

Taken from the top floor of Castle House in 1977, this photograph not only gives a fine panoramic view of the old part of the city, but also shows the P&O liner *Canberra* steaming along Southampton Water at the start of a luxury cruise.

Both taken on the same day in 1977, these photographs commemorate the visit of Queen Elizabeth II to Southampton to celebrate her Silver Jubilee. The top picture shows the Royal Yacht *Britannia* steaming along Southampton Water, while the bottom picture shows the Royal Navy escort ship that accompanied her.

Above Bar Street was pedestrianised in 1972. This view from the top of the Bargate shows how the precinct looked in its early days. Since then it has been made a permanent feature of the city and was altered in 1999 to bring it into line with the entrance to the West Quay Shopping Mall. (*Veal Collection*)

Not to be confused with the Above Bar Congregational Church, which stood on the eastern side of Above Bar Street and was destroyed in the blitz, this church is on the corner of Above Bar Street and Ogle Road, on the western side of Above Bar Street. The original church building was demolished in the 1970s and replaced by the modern church and shops that you can see here.

The 1960s saw the decline of luxury liners in Southampton but, by the 1970s, the container ships had made their first appearance. This 1970s photograph shows the early days of Southampton's successful container berth. (*Associated British Ports*)

Once the home of the Southampton Rhythm Club, a popular venue for jazz enthusiasts, the Cliff Hotel in Woolston closed in the early 1980s. The building was derelict for several years before being restored to become a block of luxury apartments. The photograph, taken in about 1987, shows the restoration work beginning.

The original Mitchell Aircraft Museum was contained in a large Nissen hut near the Marlands. This photograph, taken in the 1970s, shows it how it looked before moving to its permanent premises in Albert Road. (*Southampton Reference Library*)

Shown here in the 1970s, Maddison Street was once a street of terraced houses leading from Castle Square to the Castle Bailey. The street still exists but the old houses and Maggs' General Store on the corner were replaced by modern dwellings in about 1985. (*Veal Collection*)

One of the finest moments in Southampton's recent history was in 1982 when the P&O liner *Canberra* returned to her home port, battle scarred and rusty, from the Falklands conflict. Thousands turned out to welcome her and the troops that she carried that day. It wasn't long before she had a major refit and was back in service as a cruise liner. Sadly, the ship was scrapped in September 1997 after more than 30 years of service. (*Southern Newspapers plc*)

This view from the top floor of Castle House shows the docks and the High Street in the middle 1970s. Many ships are in port but the one most prominent is the P&O liner *Arcadia*.

New houses were built in Castle Square and Maddison Street in about 1985. Beyond the new houses you can see the Pirelli cable works, which, having been a blot on the landscape since 1914, were demolished shortly after this photograph was taken. The new West Quay Shopping Mall and Retail Park now occupies the whole of the Pirelli site.

The Hants and Dorset bus station, opposite the Civic Centre and seen here in about 1981, was demolished in 1987 to make way for the Marlands shopping mall. Few people, including me, know where to catch a bus in Southampton these days. (*Southampton Reference Library*)

Modern
Southampton

The 1930s clock tower of the Civic Centre looks extremely dated from this angle. Both built in the 1990s, on the right is the ultra-modern Skandia House while on the left, in a more traditional style, are halls of residence for students of the Southampton Institute.

A few years ago Southampton's High Street had a paucity of public houses, one after another being closed. In the middle 1990s, however, many large drink and catering retailers took over empty buildings and turned them into pubs. This photograph of the High Street shows the first of such pubs, The Standing Order, which was once the TSB. Next door is an Australian theme pub called Walkabout which is housed in the old Bank of England building. This particular photograph shows something perhaps unique to Southampton. On the left you can see part of the Royal Bank of Scotland, which used to be The Southerner public house. So the picture shows a bank that was once a pub and two pubs that were once banks. Other premises that became pubs in the 1990s were: Woolwich Building Society (Ferryman and Firkin); ABC cinema (The Square); Clarks Shoes (Hogshead); Miss Selfridge (Yates's Wine Bar); Southerngas showroom (The Old Fat Cat); Winton's Furniture Store (The Giddy Bridge) and Woodhouse's Furniture Store (The Goose and Granite).

Further along the High Street were the premises of the Poupart Fruit and Vegetable Wholesaler, which was one of the largest in the city and had stood on this site for many years before closing in the late 1990s. This photograph shows the building in 1998, shortly before it was demolished. The site has since been redeveloped and a block of luxury apartments is due to open in the autumn of 2000.

Canute's Pavilion is the focal point of Ocean Village. This photograph was taken in 1997 but Ocean Village was actually opened in the middle of the 1980s when Number 9 shed in the Eastern Docks became redundant and was converted into a mall of small shops, boutiques, bistros, bars and speciality outlets. Many units have changed use since the mall was opened but it still remains as entertaining and interesting as ever.

When Ocean Village was developed, a large yacht marina was constructed alongside. Several times the marina has been the venue for the start of the Whitbread Around-the-World race for sailing craft, an event that attracts many people to Ocean Village and its other entertainments.

The northern end of Above Bar Street, with the Above Bar shopping precinct in the foreground, early 1999. For several years the Southampton Information Bureau was in this convenient position but it was demolished in 1995, the service being removed to out-of-the-way Civic Centre Road. The mature trees on this spot were ripped out in 1999 so that the precinct could have a major refit to bring it into line with the entrance of the West Quay Shopping Mall. New saplings have been planted and they will eventually prove to be an asset to the precinct.

Looking at this photograph of Hanover Buildings on a Sunday morning early in 1999 makes it difficult to believe that it is such a busy road for traffic in the week. All the left-hand side of the road was destroyed in the blitz and rebuilt in the 1950s but most of the right-hand side is still much as it was in the late 1930s.

At a cost of £10,000,000, The Quays leisure, fitness and health centre opened on 17 June 1999 on the site of the derelict Centre 2000, the final name of the old Southampton swimming baths on the Western Esplanade. It provides a 25-metre swimming pool, a fun pool for children, a diving pool, a fitness suite and a health centre. The centre's alternative name is the Eddie Read Swimming and Diving Complex in honour of the late Eddie Read, one-time mayor of Southampton.

Before the land was reclaimed in the 1930s, the sea almost lapped the old walls of the city. Because the Western Esplanade is no longer a thoroughfare, the city council decided to make the eastern end of it look similar to how it was many years ago. As well as the models of boats typical of the sort that once used West Quay, the pavement has been laid out in different colours to imitate the water and the gravel shores that were there in days gone by.

107

Once considered the finest hotel in Southampton, the Polygon Hotel opened in about 1937 on the site of Polygon House, which was the remaining part of the development of luxury housing that was planned in Southampton's eighteenth-century 'Spa Period'. The hotel catered for many celebrities on their way through Southampton from the many liners that once docked in the port. The hotel closed for good on 31 December 1998 and the building was demolished to be replaced by luxury flats in 1999.

Southampton's only five-star hotel is the De Vere Grand Harbour Hotel on the corner of West Quay Road and the Western Esplanade. Opened in 1993, the hotel is truly luxurious and the food in the restaurant is said to be excellent. The hotel, together with the Post House Hotel on the opposite corner of West Quay Road, comes into its own during Southampton's annual boat show.

The Polygon development at the end of the eighteenth century was intended to provide people with exclusive (and expensive) houses that had beautiful views over Southampton Water. The development was not a success but some of the houses that were built at the time still exist. These two photographs show how the houses looked in 1999.

Where once luxury liners were tied up alongside 101 berth, the berth is now used mainly by container ships when the container dock further up river is full. This 1998 view shows two such large container ships waiting to be unloaded. Not far from these berths is the new cruise terminal from where P&O cruise liners embark and disembark their passengers.

This photograph, taken in 1999, shows the lower end of French Street. The street was virtually destroyed during the blitz of 1940 but some of the old buildings survived, notably the late nineteenth-century Eagle Warehouse of May and Wade, which is now used as a depository by *Southampton Cultural Services*.

One of the better shopping malls in down-town Southampton, The Marlands, was formally opened on 5 September 1991 by Mrs Gail Ronson, wife of the chairman of Heron International, the company that developed the mall. The main entrance to the mall was once Manchester Street and much of the mall is on the site of the old Hants and Dorset bus station. The developer tried to retain the atmosphere of the old street by keeping the facades of several of the houses intact. It looks attractive but the original houses that were once there were quite different from the imitations that replaced them.

Recreational and entertainment establishments grew up around the West Quay Retail Park in the late 1990s. The Radio Cafe was just one of them. Here, if you feel so inclined, you can have a drink and listen to loud music all day long.

The West Quay Retail Park opened in the middle 1990s with many well-known retailers taking over premises there. With adequate free parking, the retail park is a good place to shop, unless you want clothes or groceries. But you can buy a bike, home furniture, office equipment, baby stuff and shoes.

After the Bedford Place coach station was demolished in the late 1980s Southampton did not have a coach station as such. There was a makeshift, prefabricated coach station off the Western Esplanade for some years but few people knew where it was. It was in extremely poor condition, in spite of its short time in existence. When the plans for the West Quay development were drawn up a new, purpose-built coach station was included in those plans. The new station opened in about 1998 and is situated in a very convenient spot for tourists and students alike.

Two sports shops, a holiday supermarket and a pet-shop superstore are among the many other shops that were established in the other part of the West Quay Retail Park in the middle 1990s. This part, however, seems to be a little bit cut off from its neighbours in the main part of the retail park.

When you think that at the start of the twentieth century this area was under water, much has happened since the land was reclaimed in the 1930s. Two new hotels, the Novotel and the Ibis, opened in the early 1990s and since then McDonald's and TGI Friday's have also opened.

When the western side of Southampton was developed in the 1990s, many leisure activities also sprung up in the area. Among these was the Quayside pub, a comfortable, traditional pub which has the distinction of being the first purpose-built pub in Southampton for over 20 years. It does, however, look out of place among its ultra-modern neighbours.

Looking like a giant barn, Leisure World opened in the mid-1990s, together with the Grosvenor Casino. Among other things, the entertainment complex contains 12 separate Odeon cinemas, each showing a different programme. It also has cafés, bars, discos and computer games: all aimed at the younger generation. The Grosvenor Casino, on the other hand, offers sophisticated entertainment and gambling to those of more mature years.

Work began on the West Quay Shopping Mall in November 1997 with the demolition of buildings in Portland Terrace and the Western Esplanade, which left West Quay Road as the only direct access into the city from the west. In early 1999 it was decided to widen West Quay Road, which caused traffic chaos for several months. The top photograph shows the road works looking west while the bottom shows the road works looking east. Although now much improved, West Quay Road is still really the only direct route to the city from the west and, mainly due to the numerous traffic lights and the volume of traffic, hold-ups are still frequent.

Two different aspects of Portland Terrace show that the development of the West Quay Shopping Mall did not result in the demolition of the row of Regency houses. Although the buildings are well within the building site, they have remained intact and should blend in well with the new development when it finally opens.

The Dog and Duck in Portland Terrace started off as The Inn Centre in 1968. It must surely have been one of the most unprepossessing pubs in the country. The pub was demolished in late 1997, together with the Arundel Towers office block on the right, so that work on building the West Quay Shopping Mall could begin.

A later view of Portland Terrace shows the Dog and Duck gone and Arundel Towers no longer in existence. Like the other photographs taken at the time, this one is dominated by the mass of high cranes.

The new John Lewis department store, which is part of the West Quay Shopping Mall redevelopment, was rapidly taking shape in early 1999. The store promises to be the largest John Lewis store outside London, but it's a pity that it couldn't have retained the traditional Southampton name of Tyrrell and Green.

The medieval Catchcold Tower looks very much out of place among the forest of cranes that were busy building the West Quay Shopping Mall in early 1999.

Two views of the West Quay Shopping Mall, taken from the same spot in July 2000, show how quickly the work has progressed. The stores of John Lewis (above) and Marks & Spencer (below) are almost finished and being fitted out ready for the move from Above Bar Street in the autumn of 2000. Between the two major stores will be a Waitrose supermarket and numerous small cafés, bars and boutiques. The shopping mall will be among the largest in any city centre in the country.

Tall ships from around the world gathered together at Southampton docks in April 2000 in preparation for the Tall Ships' Race, which actually began from Plymouth. The people of Southampton, however, had the pleasure of seeing the splendid vessels before the start of the race. The tall ships left the port to sail to Plymouth just as the brand-new P&O cruise liner *Aurora* made her first visit to her home port of Southampton, ready for her maiden voyage. The photograph shows the Russian ship *Sedov*, which was on a courtesy visit to Southampton and didn't actually take part in the race.

Acknowledgements

Researching the information for this book has made me realise just how much Southampton has changed in the twentieth century. Many people have shown an interest in the project and, while I cannot thank them all individually, their help has been invaluable. However, several people must be singled out for recognition of their significant contribution because if it were not for those people, this book might never have been written.

Mr Veal was a keen local historian and photographed many Southampton scenes in the 1950s, 1960s and 1970s. When he died in 1977, his widow donated his splendid collection of photographs to the Southampton Archives Services. Where I have used a 'Veal' photograph, I have acknowledged it as being part of the Veal Collection.

Sue Woolgar and her staff at the Southampton Archives Services deserve a special mention because they went out of their way to help me track down obscure photographs of many parts of the city. Many of the photographs were commissioned by the City Council and are catalogued in the archives as SC/H2/xxx. The hundreds of photographs in the collection can be viewed by the public at the Southampton Archives Services office in the Civic Centre. Likewise David Hollingsworth of the City Reference Library gave me great help in sorting though the photographs in the Special Collections department of the library.

Other acknowledgements in this book are to Associated British Ports, National Monuments Records Centre and Southern Newspapers plc. They all helped contribute to this collection of photographs. I have made individual acknowledgements to other contributors in the photograph captions.

Special thanks are due to my wife Joyce for her patience and for checking my work for repeated words, missing words and for captions that simply didn't make sense.

Where I have been unable to locate the precise owners of photographs, after making all reasonable efforts to find them, I have acknowledged them simply as belonging to the Gallaher Collection. Photographs without any acknowledgement at all are those that I took myself; therefore the copyright is mine. Should I have inadvertently infringed anyone's copyright, then I apologise. In every case I did my best to find copyright owners, but some just eluded me completely.

Tony Gallaher, October 2000